A Girl's Guide

Take Better Selfies

Alysa Salzberg

ELDORADO INK

Eldorado Ink
PO Box 100097
Pittsburgh, PA 15233
www.eldoradoink.com

Produced by OTTN Publishing, Stockton, New Jersey

CPSIA compliance information: Batch#GG2017.
For further information, contact Eldorado Ink at info@eldoradoink.com.

First printing

1 3 5 7 9 8 6 4 2

Library of Congress Cataloging-in-Publication Data

on file at the Library of Congress
ISBN 978-1-61900-111-4 (hc)
ISBN 978-1-61900-119-0 (ebook)

About the Author: Alysa Salzberg is a writer and blogger whose work has appeared in a number of print and online publications. She holds a degree in art history from New York University and is a fan of travel, books, cookies, and funny animal videos. She lives with her husband, train-obsessed toddler, and cuddly black cat in Paris, France, where she takes lots of pictures. Some of her favorites are #nofilter group selfies featuring her family and friends.

Photo Credits: Instagram: 8 (bottom); National Aeronautics and Space Administration: 8 (top); used under license from Shutterstock, Inc.: 1, 4, 6 (right), 7, 9 (top), 10, 12, 13, 16, 19, 20, 21, 23, 25, 28, 30, 31, 32, 34, 35, 36, 41 (bottom), 43, cover; Bloomicon / Shutterstock.com: 40, 42; mar_chm1982 / Shutterstock.com: 29; Joe Seer / Shutterstock.com: 41 (top); Tinseltown / Shutterstock.com: 15; Twitter: 9 (bottom); Wikimedia Commons: 6 (left).

For information about custom editions, special sales, or premiums, please contact our special sales department at info@eldoradoink.com.

Table of Contents

Selfies at a Glance

A selfie is a photo you take of yourself, by yourself. You can take it with a camera, or using any device that has a camera such as a smartphone or tablet. You can be the only person who appears in a selfie, or you can share the spotlight with other people, animals, objects, landmarks, or landscapes.

Most of us have taken at least one selfie—and probably a lot more. But maybe you don't like the way yours turn out. Although selfies might seem simple, there are a lot of things you can do to make them look better. This book will give you tips on how to improve your selfie game.

To get to know selfies, let's find out where they come from.

THE HISTORY OF THE SELFIE

Selfies have existed for a long time. There's evidence that ancient artists depicted themselves in sketches and models, or even in finished works. But self-portraits could have appeared long before that. A recent theory suggests that prehistoric "Venus" figurines might be images of the carvers' own bodies.

During the Renaissance (ca. 1350–1600 CE), people started thinking of artists as individuals, rather than anonymous craftsmen. Many Renaissance artists added self-portraits to some of their most complex masterpieces. As time went on, it wasn't unusual for artists to feature themselves as the subject of a painting or sculpture.

What we'd consider the first selfie photograph was taken by Robert Cornelius in 1839, the year photography was officially invented. Cornelius was thinking "science" more than "selfie" when he captured his image (left), but his expression would work perfectly in a modern-day selfie. He looks serious, but curious; a little unsure, but somewhat confident.

Since Cornelius's "selfie," countless people have gone on to take pictures of themselves, especially starting around 1900, when the Kodak Brownie became the first camera available to the general public. Today, cameras in many different formats are so widely available that just about anyone can easily take a selfie. And, of course, we do. About one million selfies are shared on social media platforms every day.

WHY TAKE A SELFIE?

The word "selfie" was added to Oxford Dictionaries in 2013, and named their word of the year.

There are a lot of reasons for taking selfies, like...

> ...snapping a shot for an online profile;

> ...capturing a special moment;

> ...liking your look;

> ...celebrating your travels or the place you live;

> ... sharing happy news like a new friend, significant other, baby, or pet in your life; or

> ...showing a gift you received or something you bought.

There are also more specialized selfies. For example, a make-up artist or hair stylist might demonstrate a particular technique, or a fashionista might post a full-body selfie revealing her latest ensemble. Selfies can be used to document weight loss, muscle gain, and other changes. They can even show support for important causes, including body acceptance, political and social justice issues, and anti-bullying.

FAMOUS SELFIES THROUGH THE AGES

Many artists have created self-portraits. Rembrandt van Rijn, Vincent Van Gogh, and Frida Kahlo's numerous honest and striking ones are among the best known. Quite possibly the most creative selfies taken with a camera come from Cindy Sherman, who's been shooting herself as different people and characters since the 1970s.

Online, some selfies have become iconic, like the space selfie taken by astronaut Akihiko Hoshide in 2013 (nearly fifty years after the first space selfie, taken by Buzz Aldrin while floating above the earth in 1966); the first selfie taken with a pope (featuring Pope Francis I and a group of teen fans in 2013); and Ellen DeGeneres' group selfie taken at the 2014 Academy Awards ceremony.

Two other famous selfies weren't even taken by people. In 2011, a curious crested black macaque monkey had some fun with a camera in an Indonesian national park, snapping a shot of himself grinning. And in 2013, NASA shared the first of many selfies taken on Mars by the Mars Curiosity Rover.

Filipino politician Rodolfo Castro Fariñas (left) described this Instagram photo with Pope Francis I as the "selfie of my life."

THE BIG FOUR

There are four major factors that make a great selfie:

1. Your actual appearance
2. Angles
3. Lighting
4. Personality

Let's look at some simple ways to improve all of these in your pictures, so that your selfies will go from being "meh" to magnificent!

At the 2014 Academy Awards Ceremony, host Ellen DeGeneres gathered fellow celebrities in the audience to take a group selfie that she posted to Twitter. The picture remains the most-shared tweet in history, with nearly 3.5 million retweets, and counting.

Putting Your Best Face Forward

How to Look Great in a Selfie

Many people don't like how they look in selfies. Luckily, there are some easy things that you can do to get closer to picture perfect.

GET A GO-TO HAIRSTYLE

To take a flattering selfie, you should have a good idea of the best way to style your hair, whether permanently or just before you take your picture.

Here are some suggestions based on features you might want to play up or play down:

* Soften your chin or jaw by keeping your hair loose and flowing around your lower face. For a more permanent solution, you could consider cutting it into a bob or layers.

*   Play down your face's roundness by wearing your hair down or growing it long.
*   Minimize the size of your forehead by covering it partially or completely. You can get bangs, or comb some hair across one side for a similar effect.
*   Make your face look less long by minimizing the size of your forehead, giving your hair volume, and not wearing a high updo.
*   Accentuate your prominent cheekbones by wearing your hair up or cutting it short.

Play down your face's roundness by wearing your hair down or growing it long.

GIVE GREAT FACE

You can also play up your features with grooming and makeup. Of course, this depends on what you're allowed to do and what you're comfortable with. Some girls like to go all-out before taking a selfie. But it's also perfectly fine to choose a simpler, or even makeup-free, look. Whatever works for you, here are some very basic tips to make your face look its best in a photo:

Only shine from within. Use blotting paper or a light powder to dull shiny spots.

* Groom your eyebrows. However big or small your 'brows, make sure they're neat, with no stray hairs above or below them, and no bald patches. If you don't know how to rein them in, check out a few online video tutorials.

* Pick one feature. If you want to play up your favorite feature, make sure to stick to just that one. Otherwise, no one will know what to focus on.

* Shoulders back, face forward. So many of us end up with a double chin when we take a selfie. To stop this from happening, take your picture straight on, pushing your shoulders back and your face forward. This will elongate your neck and keep your face from leaning on it.

Get Colorful!

The colors of your clothes, accessories, and makeup can bring out your natural glow and make you look more vibrant on camera.

Teal, navy blue, purple, light pink, stone, and pure red generally look good on everyone. But if you want to find colors that are more specifically adapted to your complexion, check online or at your library for tips on how to determine your skin's undertone.

What Are You Trying to Say?

Looking your best is only part of taking an amazing selfie. You also have to know why you're taking it. Lose sight of that, and you can come off as silly, pretentious, or even mean.

For example, say you take a selfie to support a charity or important cause. A plunging neckline, pursed lips, and over-ly made-up face would make it seem like you're looking for an excuse to be sexy; the only cause you care about is your-self.

Of course, this doesn't mean you should hide who you are—after all, selfies are about you and your life.

Did You Know?

THE RISE OF BEAUTY BLOGS AND ONLINE MAKEUP TUTORIALS HAS TRANSFORMED CONTOURING FROM AN ELABORATE MAKEUP TECHNIQUE USED BY MAKEUP ARTISTS, MODELS, AND CELEBRITIES, TO A METHOD THAT'S ACCESSIBLE TO ANYONE WILLING TO LEARN. POWER TO THE (SELFIE) PEOPLE!

But life isn't always flawless or beautiful. You'd be surprised how easily most people forget about cosmetic issues when a selfie exudes real emotion.

If you have trouble showing your feelings in front of a camera, here are some things you could try:

* Think of something that made you feel very happy (or sad, silly, or thoughtful) and see if that emotion comes through.
* Play music that makes you feel a certain way.
* Smize. Coined by model Tyra Banks, this term means, "smile with your eyes." It doesn't have to be limited to smiling, however. Basically, smizing means showing emotion with your eyes, so that you don't look flat, awkward, or disengaged in a picture.

How do you smize? The easiest way is to inhale dramatically while looking at the camera. Model Tyra Banks also suggests focusing on the camera and pretending it's someone you really love or hate. If the results aren't perfect, practice in a mirror to get your smize on point.

SELFIE "DON'TS"

Some types of selfie have become common—as well as hated or laughable. For example, bathroom mirror selfies that include the toilet should be avoided. Funeral selfies are another "don't." Rules are meant to be broken, but it's hard to think of a context where disrespecting the dead and their loved ones is a good thing. In fact, any selfie that involves disrespect or suffering is generally a no-no.

Some poses are also cliché, like the extreme plunging angle or the notorious "duck face." Then again, when it comes to duck face, it depends on who you ask. Selfie "expert" Kim Kardashian, for example, swears by this pose. But generally it's best to avoid this expression, especially in a picture where you don't want to be distracting or silly. A more subtle way to achieve a similar effect is the Olsen twins' technique of saying "Prune" as you take your picture. Or try "sparrow face" instead—open your eyes wide and slightly part your lips.

Show Your Whole Self

The Full-Body Selfie

Now you know some ways to make your face look great. But what if you want to take a full-body selfie? In that case, your outfit should, above all, make you feel confident and beautiful. Once you've got that down, you can also use your clothes to bring out your best features and hide the ones you don't like.

There aren't features that you have to hide or flatter. Your photo should reflect who you are. But most of us have body parts we're less confident about than others, and if that's something that's keeping you from liking how you look in your selfies, there are ways to play them down. Here are some simple solutions to common complaints:

* To look slimmer, wear dark colors and stand with your ankles crossed.

* To make your upper arms look smaller, wear either a jacket or top with long sleeves, or shirts with fun, voluminous sleeves like batwing or butterfly wing. Avoid short sleeves that end at the thickest part of your arm.

* To make your shoulders look smaller, wear a dark top with a v-neck cut and/or sleeves or thick straps. In a full body selfie, balance it with light-colored or patterned bottoms. If you like skirts, try a flared cut.

* To hide belly fat, try wearing a top that's loose around that area—or opt for a colorful scarf that falls over your belly.

* To conceal "cankles," wear pants, calf-high boots, or black tights, or a skirt that stops at your knee. With shorter bottoms, wear shoes with a heel.

* To give yourself some curves, cinch your waist with a belt or wear a fitted top or jacket. Or put a hand on either side of the narrowest part of your waist and draw your fingers gently towards each other (but never meeting), creating a cinched-in look from nothing.

Try to check how your clothes photograph before you take the picture. Some fabrics that look solid will seem to magically turn opaque or even transparent when you take a photo, especially if you're using a flash. Black clothes can be especially deceptive.

TAKE A STANCE

Now that you know how to dress for your full-body selfie, the next step is how to pose. Here are some ideas:

* A fraction of yourself. Most of the time, full-body selfies are most flattering when you're turned slightly to the left or right, rather than facing the camera straight on.

* Hand on hip. Putting your free hand on your hip can make your arm look smaller, especially if you angle yourself slightly to one side.

* Hip jut. When taking a full-body mirror selfie, aficionados like Kylie Jenner face the mirror and slightly jut out the hip below their hand that's holding the camera. This adds curves and interesting movement to the selfie.

* Use your legs. Crossing them at the ankle makes you look slimmer. Slightly extending one leg to the side will keep you from looking boxy or boring. Bend one knee towards the camera to give interesting depth to your photo. Or just have fun—for example, raise one leg, bending it so that the sole of your foot is leaning against the knee of your other leg.

In addition to the traditional formats, there are lots of other kinds of selfies, including the foot selfie (a picture of your feet in an unusual or special place), belfie (butt selfie), action selfie (taken while doing something like bungee jumping), and the space selfie (taken by astronauts in space—really!).

FACE THE FACTS

In the last chapter, we talked about your face. But when it comes to a full-body selfie, this is now only part of the picture. Focus more on your overall pose and look, rather than your facial expression. Most people look at their phone or camera while taking their selfie in the mirror, but if you want to add a little personality, an article on EnkiVillage.com gives an interesting suggestion: Make a slight smirk.

HANDS-ON OR HANDS-FREE?

Most full-body selfies are going to be taken in front of a mirror. Some people call this cliché, but let's face it—it's easy, and even Instagram stars and celebrities do it.

Still, if you really hate mirror selfies, there are alternatives. One is using a timer. If your device doesn't already have one, you can download a timer app. Another option is using a remote shutter—a small remote connected to your device by Bluetooth. Or choose an app like CamMe or Camera Plus, which set off your phone or tablet's camera button based on a hand gesture you make.

When taking a mirror selfie, avoid clutter in the background that will distract from the shot.

Using a timer or remote shutter gives you some additional options for full-body selfie poses, such as the following:

* The hand-on-hip alternative. In an article on Beauty Editor.ca, photographer Dallas Curow suggests leaning slightly back on one leg and drawing your shoulders back. Place your hands on your thighs.

* Walk. Walking into the shot will make you look natural, and if your full-body selfie is celebrating your OOTD (Outfit of the Day), it will show your clothes in motion.

Lighting and Angles

Basic Techniques Everyone Should Know

Looking your best is a great start to taking a great selfie. But any selfie aficionado will tell you that when it comes to your physical appearance, two other things are just as important—lighting and angles. If the lighting in your selfie is too bright, it can wash out your features or highlight things you don't want to show off. If the lighting is too low, you'll look like a shadow of yourself.

Here are some tips for finding the best light:

*   Go natural. The best kind of light for a selfie is ambient and natural. If you can, take your selfie outdoors, or in a room that's evenly lit by natural light.
*   Choose yellow and white. If you can't use natural light, try to find an indoor spot with lightbulbs that mix white and yellow light.

* Don't turn your back. Generally, if there's one specific source of light (a window, the sun, etc.), you want it to be in front of you, not behind you.

* Don't be flashy. If you can, avoid using a flash, which will make your features look harsher or could make your clothes appear transparent. Using a flash could also leave a distracting reflection in a mirror or on a bright wall surface behind you, or could leave you with "redeye."

* Use the back camera. If your phone has a front and back camera, try using the back one. You won't be able to see your screen, but the back camera is higher resolution than the front one.

Turning your back to the main light source can result in your photo being washed out, with details becoming indistinct.

THE PROPER ANGLE

The angle is the direction that you take your picture from. But before you start trying different angles out, you should get to know your face. Most of us have one side (usually the left) that photographs best. Many stars, models, and social media celebrities spend hours in front of the mirror testing what works for them. So take your time and discover your best side and the angle that compliments it. To help you get started, here are some camera angle tips that tend to help most people:

* From above. Holding the camera slightly above your face makes your eyes look bigger and the rest of your face slimmer. Be careful not to make the angle too plunging, however. This is an internet cliché that will give your photo an immature or attention-seeking vibe.

* Three-quarters. Turn your best side to the camera at a three-quarter angle.

* Straight on with your head tilted to one side. This is a favorite of many celebrities. It gives your selfie some personality and shows off your cheekbones and eyes.

In general, most expert photographers suggest avoiding low angles. A selfie taken from slightly below the chin can look good for a select few people, but most of us should choose other options for everyday selfies.

Angles can also send a message. For example, if you want to give an impression of strength, taking a photo straight on, or even from slightly below (as long as the angle isn't distractingly unflattering) will make you look more powerful. Or, if you want to look demure, cute, or softer, taking a photo from above is the way to go.

Studies have shown that humans seem to naturally have a preference for the left side of the face. You can see this in portraits from as early as the 14th century, as well as in selfies posted online today.

ANGLES FOR FULL-BODY SELFIES

What about full-body selfies? If you're holding the camera and taking a mirror selfie, the angle is more or less going to be straight on. To make the shot look better, concentrate on lighting and poses.

If you're using a timer, remote shutter, or selfie stick, remember that while a selfie from below could be unflattering, it might also be a way to convey power or a sense of being larger-than-life. If you don't want to do that angle, and if you're worried that taking a shot from above may not show all of you, a straight-on angle is probably best.

ACCESSORIES THAT CAN IMPROVE YOUR SELFIES

Some accessories can help you take even better selfies. Take camera lights for smartphones, like celebrity favorites the LuMee and Ty-Lite phone cases. These cases are only available for newer iPhone and Samsung model smartphones. But light attachments compatible with older-generation phones exist, too. Do an online search to find one for your phone.

Another useful selfie accessory is a remote shutter, a small remote control that connects to your device via Bluetooth, letting you take a hands-free selfie. Since you won't be holding your device, a tripod could be a good idea. There are a lot of different kinds out there, from tall, professional-grade models, to small, easy-to-carry flexible ones.

And who could forget selfie sticks? They may get made fun of, but plenty of selfie aficionados swear by them, and anyway, why worry about not being able to include all of your pals or surroundings in a shot? Some sticks use a remote to take the photo, while others incorporate Bluetooth or an integrated button.

Background Information

What to Include, What Not to Include

When taking a selfie, never neglect what's going on behind you. Your background could work for you, or it could totally ruin your picture. Unless you're taking a selfie to show yourself in a particular place, the background may not seem important. But think about it:

* A messy room or bathroom makes people say, "How clean is this person?"

* A person or animal doing something funny or weird (intentionally or not) behind you will definitely get all the attention.

* Sexual, obscene, or controversial items, symbols, and posters can detract focus from you and will give an impression that may not really represent who you are—or who you'll be years from now, when people can still find the selfie on social media.

* Taking a selfie in an inappropriate place or situation will probably just make people feel bad—or make them think badly of you. Funerals, religious sites, crime scenes, memorials, solemn ceremonies, accidents, disasters, war zones, and fires are definitely not good selfie backgrounds.

Another issue to think about with the background of your selfie is how much personal information it might give away. Avoid selfie backgrounds that show the street you live on or the number of your house. Don't allow personal documents to appear in the background of your photos—even if they're far away, you never know who's looking and who might be able to zoom in. Money or other signs of wealth might tempt people to steal from you or your family. And never include illegal or dangerous items, such as drugs, weapons, alcohol, or cigarettes. Even if you possess or use these things legally, not everyone looking at the picture will know that. Such photos could become a problem for you years from now, if a future employer sees the picture somewhere.

Have fun—but be aware that when you post a selfie on the internet, people may draw conclusions about you.

FINDING A GREAT SELFIE BACKGROUND

Now that you know what to avoid, here are some tips for making the most of your selfie background:

* Consider cropping. Unless the background is interesting, important, or really looks great, consider cropping most of it out, so that you're the star.

* Stay neutral. Remember that most selfies are about you (and whoever else you might be taking the picture with), not a distracting background. Try standing in front of a solid wall or a nondescript natural scene.

If you take a selfie in front of a painting or fresco, please don't use the flash—the bright light from cameras can damage paint.

* Have fun with colors. If you're taking a full-body selfie to show your outfit, try posing against a bright, solid colored background to bring out the colors in your clothes. Feeling bold? Try a uniform pattern, like bricks, that could contrast or play up your look.

* If it's shiny, don't flash. If you're standing behind a reflective surface, like shiny tiles, your flash could end up making an unwanted cameo in the photo.

LET THE BACKGROUND SHARE THE SPOTLIGHT

Of course, some selfies are just as much about a location as they are about you. Whether you're on your dream vacation or celebrating your favorite place in town, here are some things to think about if you want the background to share your space:

* Play with angles. Sometimes, you can have a lot of fun and show a well-known site or spot in a new, but recognizable way, making your selfie even more interesting.

According to a 2015 study by Attractiontix.co.uk, the three most popular places for travelers to take selfies are the Eiffel Tower in Paris, Disney World in Orlando, Florida, and the Burj Khalifa skyscraper in Dubai.

* Do something. Jump in the air, strike a fun or interesting pose, or even capture yourself as you stroll into the frame (these suggestions are easier if you have a timer, remote shutter, or selfie stick). Just make sure what you're doing goes with the place you're photographing. A solemn religious site or monument may not be the best place for a selfie at all, let alone one where you look like you're jumping for joy.

Adding activity to your selfie can make it more interesting.

* Get in position. To show a large area like a beach or canyon, place yourself near the edge of the frame (usually the right side of the picture works best). Or put yourself in the center of the shot if you still want to be the star. A specific building, on the other hand, might make for a better fit over one of your shoulders. Some travel photography fans even suggest taking a selfie from a vantage point above the place of interest—for example, a hill or balcony overlooking it. Be creative—and most of all, be sure that where you're standing is safe and that you don't walk backwards.

Squad Goals

Photos With Your Favorite People or Pets

Group selfies let you get a picture of your whole crew that looks more natural than a posed shot taken by someone else. They can also show the closeness (or silliness) between you and your bestie, significant other, relative, or pet.

They're a great way to share the love—but taking one that you'll love requires some work:

* Check yourself. Group selfies aren't just about you, but you still want to look your best. Remember to prepare your look as much as possible, and strike a flattering pose (but still fit in with the mood and look of the rest of your squad).

* Look out for your friends. If your group selfie is going to be shared on social media, make sure no one looks embarrassing or weird, or has their eyes closed.

Various companies and individuals have tried to come up with a catchy name for a selfie featuring more than one person, including "groufie," "usie," and "wefie." For now, however, none of them has been able to displace "group selfie" as the most popular term.

* Consider using a selfie stick. Sometimes, it's the only way to fit everyone in the picture.

* Represent. If your group selfie represents a company or organization, be sure there aren't any lewd gestures, controversial details, or anything else that's inappropriate.

* Be creative! If you want to make your group selfie stand out, have everyone jump towards the camera at the top of the selfie stick, or strike different, silly poses. You could also use funny or significant props (or add effects like that in later, with an app). For example, for a vacation shot, you could pose with suitcases or things you bring to the beach.

SHOW THE LOVE: COUPLES SELFIES

There are some selfie "co-star" situations where a few more rules and ideas apply if you want the picture to come out great.

For example, the best couples selfies show each person's individual personality, as well as the "vibe" of your relationship. If you guys like to goof around, why not pose with funny props, make funny faces, or strike strange poses? If you're more romantic, face each other and look into each other's eyes, or turn your best sides to the camera and look off into the distance, in the same direction.

But maybe you just want a classic shot that will show your feelings for each other without being too flashy. One nice couples selfie pose you'll often see is where Person 1 holds the camera straight on or slightly raised, and smiles. Person 2 is behind Person 1 with their arms around them, and either looking directly at the camera, as well, or kissing Person 1 on the cheek.

Whatever you decide, the most important rule of couples selfies is to show yourselves at your best. If you look great in one shot but your significant other doesn't, it's probably not the best one to share on social media. Remember, too, that a couples selfie you post online probably shouldn't get too personal. Imagine you guys are starring in a PG-rated romantic comedy, not a raunchy, R-rated flick.

THE WILD BUNCH

Selfies with a baby, toddler, or pet are probably the hardest kind to take, since your co-star(s) can't follow directions. Here are some things to keep in mind:

* Timing is everything. If a baby is cranky, a toddler can't sit still, or your cat's hiding from the vacuum, it's probably not the best time to scoop them up and try to get a great picture.

* Get their attention. Toddlers may be interested in looking at your device's screen, making things pretty easy. For younger babies or pets, try jiggling a little toy or pet treat just above where you want them to look.

* Make them laugh. Babies and toddlers find a lot of things to laugh about. If you know a song or sound that does the trick, go for it and then click away as they're cracking up!

* Keep clicking. It's rare to get a great picture the first time you attempt to take any kind of selfie, let alone one with such unpredictable co-stars. So keep clicking that camera button. Bonus: You may capture some more unexpected, natural poses, too.

* Let them take the lead. A toddler won't stop pouting? Why not try to make an expression just like his? Your dog won't look at your phone? Try looking in the same direction. Your newborn niece won't open her eyes? Close yours and take a sleeping

Use your device's burst (high speed) mode to capture a laughing baby or toddler's movement without blurring.

selfie! You won't get the picture you were planning on, but you'll probably end up with something a lot more unique.

Most importantly, be kind! You're trying to take the picture because you love this person or animal sharing it with you. If a baby, toddler, or pet doesn't want to do something, never put them in a situation where they're afraid, in danger, or upset. Snapping a selfie takes a few seconds, but negative feelings can last for a long time.

POSING WITH PROPS

Props can add personality to a photo. For example, photo booth props—paper cut-outs of things like glasses, hats, and beards on long sticks—can make for a whimsical feel. Or, if you want to be more modern about it, use a photo editing app or website to add similar details to your selfies after you've taken them.

Sometimes, props can be the reason you're taking the selfie. Let the object share the space with you. For example, if you're showing off a new pair of earrings, try taking your picture from a 3/4 angle, so that we see one earring in front of the camera, then your face, then (if the earrings are dangly), maybe a little bit of the other one. If you want to show off a book (maybe even this one!), take some shots of you "reading" it.

Food is another common selfie prop, but it can be hard to bite into something and still look good. Hold it near your mouth, instead. To give some personality to the photo, try expressing how happy (or unhappy) you are that you're about to eat the food.

SELFIE SAFETY RISKS

Selfies can be fun, but they also come with risks. People have been blackmailed, fired, or publicly shamed because of an inappropriate photo. Before you take or share a selfie, always consider what the outcome might be if everyone in the world could see it.

This also holds true for group selfies. Avoid posting things that could be incriminating or embarrassing for, or reveal too much information about, friends and family. And if you're taking a group selfie with kids, make sure you ask their parents if it's okay for you to post (and tag) them on your social media profiles.

Even taking selfies can be dangerous. In 2015, news outlets reported that more people had died while taking selfies than from shark attacks that year. A frequently cited Wikipedia list reveals that typical causes of death by selfie include taking one while driving a car, falling from a cliff, or risky behavior like climbing onto trains.

Before you take a selfie, be aware of your surroundings. Avoid walking backwards, especially at high elevations. And don't take risks. Even if you end up with a cool, unforgettable photo, you might not survive the experience!

Photo Development

Editing Your Selfie

Even selfie masters aren't always satisfied with a good picture. They often rely on photo editing tools to make their pictures perfect. Sometimes, all it takes is a small change to make your selfie flawless. Most devices that allow you to take pictures include at least basic editing functions like zooming, cropping, straightening, and adjusting brightness.

If your device doesn't do these, or if you want to do even more, you can download an app, upload your selfie to an online photo editor, or even buy professional-grade software like Adobe Photoshop.

Before you start editing your selfie, it's a good idea to make a copy of the photo. Use the copy to upload and edit. This way, you'll still have the original if you end up not liking the way your edits turned out.

One very important thing to know: photos you upload onto just about any editing app or website can be used by the site or app in any way they choose. So don't upload anything that you wouldn't be comfortable with other people seeing.

SOFTWARE, APPS, AND SITES TO KNOW

Here are some popular photo editing apps, software, and websites:

* Photoshop (www.photoshop.com): The classic photo editing tool, used by professionals and amateurs alike. Photoshop can do everything from balancing skin tone to changing someone's silhouette. There are a variety of versions of it (including app versions) available. Unlike most of the other options on this list, most Photoshop products aren't free.

* Instagram (www.instagram.com): Not only does Instagram let you share your selfies with the world (or just to select people, if you prefer); it also works as a basic photo editing tool.

* Pixlr (https://pixlr.com/): This free editing software is sort of like a simplified version of Photoshop. Additional apps or membership options may cost money.

Instagram is known for its filters.

* VSCO Cam (https://vsco.co/): Professional-level photography editing tools, as well as a community you can run your finished selfies by!

* FaceTune (www.facetuneapp.com): This easy-to-use tool lets you tweak facial features, including teeth whiteness, wrinkles, pimples, and hair that flew out of your ponytail.

* YouCam Perfect (www.perfect-corp.com/): Another option that lets you alter physical features, including your legs and waistline. You can also remove the background of your selfie. Other apps from this company let you add makeup and nail designs.

* Perfect365 (http://perfect365.arcsoft.com/): Similar to FaceTune, this app lets you clear blemishes and touch up different features. You can also do contouring and apply different makeup and hair styles to your selfie. Not only does it sound like fun; the Kardashian sisters seem to swear by it, so it's legit.

Kim Kardashian is considered the "Queen of Selfies" because of the large number of photos that she takes of herself. Kardashian even published a book of her selfies in 2015.

Photo Filters

Even if they don't edit their selfies, many people use filters to enhance them. In the digital photography world, filters are software that instantly applies a certain color scheme or style to a digital photo. Filters can make a picture look richer or more intense in color, or like something from an old-school camera. They can give an image one overriding color, or just add a light glow to it. They can make an image sharp or romantically softer, and so much more.

Instagram's popular #NoFilter hashtag isn't always used honestly. A recent study found that 11 percent of #NoFilter-tagged photos were, in fact, edited in some way.

If you want to go beyond filters and get creative in a different way, try apps like Prisma (http://prisma-ai.com/), which will make your selfie look like a painted or drawn portrait, or PIP Camera (www.fotoable.com/en/), which makes a selfie look like it's inside of something (a bottle, a tear drop, and so on).

Easy on the Editing!

The key to an amazing selfie is not going overboard. You've probably seen examples of editing or filter "fails." The biggest culprits include cropping yourself into a background that obviously looks fake, altering your body to unrealistic proportions, and increasing or erasing curves without realizing the background now looks warped.

Another photo editing no-no is using a filter when you may not need to. Think about it: Does that fun group selfie you took of you and your friends at a football game really need a glowing, romantic light added to it?

Before you start editing your selfie, here are some things to consider:

1. Is there a good reason to edit it or use a filter?
2. Are the lighting, centering, and background already good?
3. Do you like how you look in the untouched photo?

June 21 was recently declared National Selfie Day. The next time it comes around, share one of your favorite selfies on social media!

Based on your answers, consider taking the #nofilter route. After all, in the best selfies, what we notice and appreciate most is personality, not absolute perfection.

PICTURE PERFECT

That's what it really comes down to. No matter how good you look, no matter how perfect your angle and lighting situation, if your personality doesn't shine, it's still not going to be a great selfie. So laugh, make a natural smile—or even a goofy face!

It's estimated that more than a million selfies are taken every day. The tips in this book should help you take great-looking pictures. But letting your inner self shine is what will make your selfies really stand out!

Glossary

ambient light—natural or soft artificial light that fills a space evenly, without bright spots or shadows. This is generally the best kind of light for selfies.

angle—the camera angle depends on where you hold your camera. For example, you can take a selfie with a plunging angle when you hold the camera far above your head. The result is an image of you as if the viewer were looking down at you.

Burst mode—Also called "high speed camera", this is either a function built into your camera or device, or a type of app you can download. It allows your camera to shoot photos nonstop, capturing movement without blurriness.

crop—to cut out part of a photo.

duck face—pursing your lips together so that they make an exaggerated pout, accentuating your cheekbones. In some cases, duck face can look flattering, but most of the times it comes off as a silly selfie cliché, especially if it's done in an inappropriate setting.

filter—a special lens that fits over a regular camera lens in order to capture light and colors differently. Also refers to a digital effect that can be used on photos to do things like brighten, enhance, saturate, or otherwise manipulate colors and light, or to add props, disguises, and other fun elements to a photo or video.

iconic—something that is well-known and respected.

OOTD—Outfit Of The Day. A popular term (and, usually, hashtag) with social media fashionistas, but anyone can use it if they're feeling their look and want to share a selfie of it online.

remote shutter—a small handheld device that allows you to activate your camera's shutter (or the button on your phone or tablet) from a distance. A remote shutter may also be connected by a cable to high-end or professional cameras.

smize—a term coined by model Tyra Banks, "smize" means "smile with your eyes." In other words, show expression with your eyes, which will make your photo more compelling. Two simple ways to smize are by focusing on the camera and imagining a strong emotion (for example, thinking about a person you love or hate), or looking directly at the camera and inhaling dramatically.

sparrow face—a more subtle version of duck face. Sparrow face is accomplished by keeping your eyes wide and slightly parting your lips.

squad—the people you're close to and hang out with.

three-quarter angle—Considered one of the most flattering angles for a face or full body selfie, this means turning yourself slightly to the left or right so that three-quarters of your face and/or body is visible to the camera.

timer—a device, feature, or app that allows you to delay a picture for a few seconds so that you can get into the shot. Most digital cameras and some phones and tablets come equipped with a timer. Otherwise, you can download a timer app.

#nofilter (also written "#Nofilter" or "#NoFilter")—a hashtag popularized on the social media site Instagram, this means the photo you're sharing has not been edited or retouched. The term has become so well known that you can also see it used as an adjective without a hashtag ("no filter").

Further Reading

Ang, Tom. *Photography: The Definitive Visual History*. New York: DK, 2014.

Bell, Julian. *500 Self-Portraits*. London: Phaidon Press, 2004.

Fox, Rossi. *The Selfie Journal: A Photo Journal Of 101 Selfies To Take And Collect*. London: Rossi Fox, 2015.

Hall, James, Wolfgang Ullrich, and Pierre Vaisse. *Facing the World: Self-Portraits (and Selfies) from Rembrandt to Ai Weiwei*. Ghent, Belgium: Snoeck Publishers, 2016.

Kardashian West, Kim. *Selfish*. New York: Rizzoli, 2015.

Strickland, Carol. *The Annotated Mona Lisa: A Crash Course in Art History from Prehistoric to Post-Modern*. 2nd ed. Kansas City, Missouri: Andrews McMeel Publishing, 2007.

Internet Resources

https://www.buzzfeed.com/kristinchirico/a-model-taught-us-how-to-not-suck-at-selfies-and-it-actually?utm_term=.nq3OOrK520#.xwq88rdBZ5

This is a great, short list of advice from model Tess Holliday on the art of selfie-taking.

http://www.dailymail.co.uk/femail/article-2463542

Everything you need to know about a subtle alternative to the "duck face" pose.

http://www.wikihow.com/Choose-Colors-That-Flatter-Skin-Tone

This guide will give you the basics on how to determine your skin's undertone and what colors will look best on you.

http://www.enkivillage.com/how-to-take-a-mirror-selfie.html

Helpful, detailed information about taking great full-body mirror selfies.

www.scienceofpeople.com/2015/01/take-perfect-selfie

This intriguing article, "How to Take the Perfect Selfie," gets into the science of selfies—things like the subliminal meaning of angles, and what a real smile actually is.

https://en.wikipedia.org/wiki/List_of_selfie-related_injuries_and_deaths

Although Wikipedia isn't usually considered a definitive source, this list has been cited by multiple reputable media outlets. It provides a few harsh lessons about the dangers of taking selfies.

Index

Numbers in **bold italic** refer to captions.